Written By: Anna DiGilio

All rights reserved. No part of this publication may be reproduced, distributed, or transmitted in any form or by any means, including photocopying, recording, or other electronic or mechanical methods, without the prior written permission of the publisher, except in the case of brief quotations embodied in critical reviews and certain other noncommercial uses permitted by copyright law.

For permission requests, write to the publisher:
Laprea Publishing
info@lapreapublishing.com

Website: www.GuidedReaders.com

ISBN: 978-1-64579-182-9

© 2019 Anna DiGilio

Photo Credits:
Cover, Title Page (top, bottom), 7 (bottom), 11 (top, bottom): Depositphotos; Lifeonwhite. 3: Depositphotos; Krivosheevv. 4 (top), 10 (bottom left): Depositphotos; Saharrr. 4 (bottom): Depositphotos; Janefromyork. 4 (background): Depositphotos; Artmim. 5: Guided Readers; Anna DiGilio. 6 (top): Depositphotos; Jenoche. 6 (bottom left): Depositphotos; StudioM. 6 (bottom right): Depositphotos; Klanneke. 7 (top): Depositphotos; Ksena32. 8 (top): Depositphotos; Oneinchpunch. 8 (bottom): Depositphotos; Kwanchaichaiudom. 9 (top): Depositphotos; Mihtiander. 9 (bottom left): Depositphotos; Tiverylucky. 9 (bottom right): Depositphotos; Klanneke. 10 (top left): Depositphotos; Mdworschak. 10 (top right): Depositphotos; SimpleFoto. 10 (bottom right): Depositphotos; Vviz-arch. 12 (top): Depositphotos; Martynova.Katie. 12 (bottom): Depositphotos; CroMarry.

TABLE OF CONTENTS

How Are Goats and Sheep Alike?.........Page 5

How Are Goats and Sheep Different?..Page 7

A Loving Friend..Page 12

Glossary..Page 13

Goats and sheep look alike. They sound alike. They're on farms. They're in petting zoos. They are the same. But they're different, too.

How Are Goats and Sheep Alike?

Goats and sheep have <u>hooves</u>. They have stomachs with four parts inside! Each part is like a room. It holds food. One room has food that was eaten fast. It gets sent back up to be chewed some more. This is called <u>cud</u>. Goats and sheep chew cud.

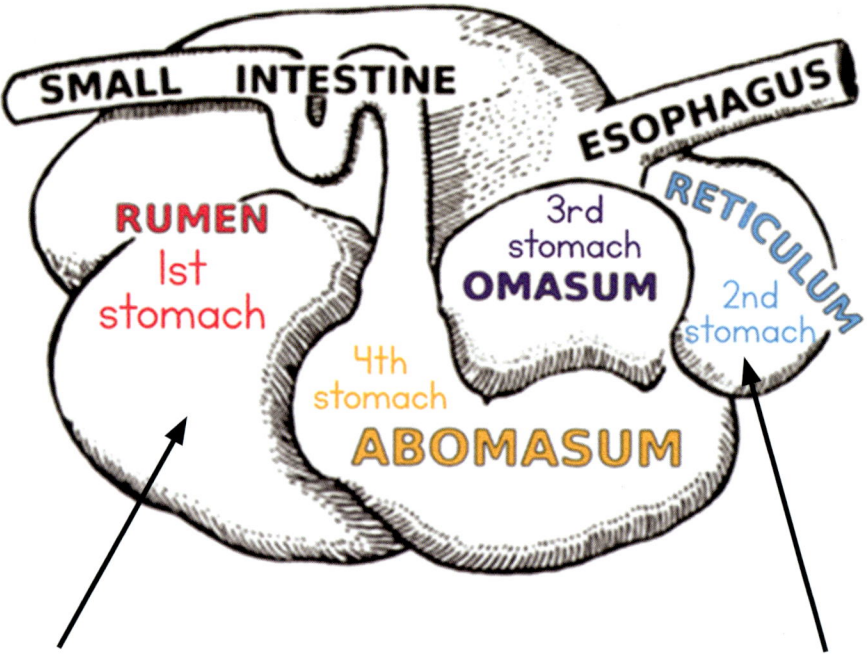

After the goat or sheep swallows, the chewed grass goes to the first two "rooms" in its stomach called the rumen and the reticulum. That is where it is broken down into cud. The goat or sheep brings the cud up and chews it again.

A farmer is milking a goat.

Goats and sheep give milk. You can drink it. It makes cheese.

Goat cheese

A farmer is milking a sheep.

How Are Goats and Sheep Different?

How are these animals different? Sheep have curly hair. It's thick. It's called wool. Goats have <u>fine</u> hair. It is like fur. Both are used to make clothes. Wool is warmer.

Notice the difference in their hair.

Goats are friendly! They like to be near you. They want to see what you're doing! Sheep do not. They stay away. They want to be with other sheep.

Goats will eat whatever they can find.

Goats love to eat. They'll eat anything. They eat grass. They eat old cans! They eat old boots! Sheep do not do that. They can't. They'd get sick. They eat soft grass.

This sheep is eating grass.

A goat will even eat a straw hat!

A Loving Friend

Sheep and goats are cute. They are friends to humans. They feed us. They keep us warm. We should show them both love for all they do for us!

GLOSSARY

<u>cud</u>
a portion of food that returns from the first stomach to the mouth to chew a second time

<u>fine</u>
very thin in texture

<u>hooves</u>
the hard covers on the feet of some mammals such as horses, deer, sheep, or goats

PREFACE

This book is designed to provide a general introduction to the principles of interactive computing and a comprehensive practical guide to the programming language BASIC.

It is felt that there is much to commend in BASIC for the beginner to computer programming who is primarily interested in using a computer for his own discipline rather than in becoming a professional programmer. BASIC is primarily designed for terminal usage, is easy to learn, and has comprehensive facilities for the solution of numerical problems.

This book is primarily intended for scientists, engineers, statisticians and other research workers who wish to acquire quickly a knowledge of computer programming to assist their work in their own subject. It is thought that the use of BASIC would be very relevant to their requirements in view of the growing use of terminal facilities by research workers. Undergraduates and members of upper forms of secondary schools who have access to a computer terminal will also find this book appropriate to their needs. It is thought also that the later chapters may be of assistance to the professional programmer who wishes to learn BASIC quickly.

The common features of BASIC have been stressed throughout so that this book will be of use to workers on a great variety of computers which have BASIC compilers, and is independent of any particular type of hardware.

The emphasis throughout is on practical programming so that the book can be used as a manual of self-instruction. There are many examples of programs and the exercises at the ends of many chapters are accompanied by suggested solutions. It is hoped that the reader will gain access to a terminal or to a computer he can use in the early stages of his study of the chapters devoted to BASIC. Since there is a great deal more in programming than mere coding of language statements, a chapter is devoted to pre-coding activities and the problems of program testing.

No knowledge of higher mathematics is needed for the comprehension of the text. Character handling has been discussed with a view to assisting readers with non-numerical interests to utilise the power of the computer for their own needs. The last chapter discusses the transition from BASIC to FORTRAN. Many users who commence programming in BASIC may wish to extend their knowledge to include the elements of FORTRAN, which is the most widely used high-level computer language for scientific and technical purposes.

I would like to express my thanks in particular to Keith Short of Computer Technology Ltd for assistance in testing the suggested solutions to the exercises; to Elaine Denyer, Nora McDermott, Jenny Pike and Mary Simkin for expert typing assistance, and to the staff of the publishers for their helpfulness and guidance.

P.C.S.